RAIN VIOLENT

RAIN VIOLENT

ANN SPIERS
poet

BOLINAS FRANK
artist & calligrapher

Empty Bowl
Anacortes, Washington

Empty Bowl, founded in 1976 as a cooperative letterpress publisher, has produced periodicals, broadsides, literary anthologies, collections of poetry, and books of Chinese translations. As of 2018, our mission is to publish the work of writers who share Empty Bowl's founding purpose, "literature and responsibility," and its fundamental theme, the love and preservation of human communities in wild places.

ISBN 978-1-7341873-9-7
Library of Congress Control Number: 2021936205

Empty Bowl Press
2232 West Valley Road
Chimacum, WA 98325
www.emptybowl.org
editor@emptybowl.org

Cover art by Bolinas Frank
Cover & Book design by Tonya Namura

ACKNOWLEDGEMENTS

Thank you to the journals below. Some poems appear in different versions and under different titles.

Barrow Street: "Hurricane." 2020.

Bricolage: "Thunder with Dust Storm," "Wind Out of the North." 2018.

Canary: "Weather Station on the Coast," "Weather Station on a Plain." 2018-9.

Hummingbird: "Dust Raised by Wind," "Fresh Snow." 2017.

Kudzu: "Dust Devils," "Eddies," "Snow Granular." 2015.

Modern Haiku: "Rain Freezing." 2015.

Peasandcues Press: Broadside "Rain Violent." 2015.

Water Water Everywhere: "Clouds Dissolving," "Ground Flooded," "No Clouds," "Stratocumulus Not from Spread of Cumulus." 2015.

Written River: "Calm," "Ground Covered with Thawing Snow," "Haze," "Sky Overcast," "Visibility Reduced by Smoke." 2016.

Yakima Poetry Pole: "Thunder Heard." Undated.

CONTENTS

I

II

III

IV

Each poem's symbol and title are from the International Weather Symbols and other weather symbols. Weather watchers use them to record present climate conditions at local weather stations. These visual displays are used worldwide by other ground stations, ships, airplanes, and meteorological centers to record weather data.

To Ahmalie Frank and Adi Frank
Be champions for the earth,
quietly or noisily, peacefully or wildly.

INTERNATIONAL WEATHER SYMBOLS

Each poem in *Rain Violent* is headed with a symbol and its title from the International Weather Symbols. These symbols depict the surface weather such as drizzle, fog, rain, and thunder. My hope is that the symbols inject the poems with depth, counterpoint, and link to specific weather phenomena as the poem details today's climate crisis.

The International Weather Symbols are the visual code used to depict surface conditions observed at local weather stations worldwide. The World Meteorological Organization (WMO) oversees this coding system. The data illustrated include cloud type and cover, temperature, precipitation, wind speed and direction, atmospheric pressure, precipitation type and amount. Plotted on a page, the visuals use a prescribed placement of symbols outside a central circle to record surface weather conditions at one time and one place.

The complexity of the maps ranges from eight to many notations, depending on the station's purpose and instrumentation. Observations are made once or twice a day or, given today's capabilities, second to second.

These stationary weather stations, numbering in the tens of thousands, are sited in citizen scientists' backyards and fields, on sea buoys and ships, and at universities and meteorological institutions. Making further data available for surface weather maps are today's computer systems and software, affordable instrumentation, open reporting systems, satellites, and GIS.

Weather hobbyists have been the most numerous data recorders and sharers over time. The data are used by researchers as well as by airplane pilots, sea captains, ground transports, and citizens to chart the safest course.

In the mid-1800's, inventors added to the collection of instruments measuring weather. This growing ability to gather weather data was available and affordable, as it is today, to both amateur and professional weather watchers. In the 1840's, weather watchers used another new invention, the telegraph, to transmit observations to regional, national, and global agencies. Combined, the data produce weather maps of wider geographical areas. With the new source of data, newspapers printed weather maps; weather forecasting emerged from the compilations. By 1941, global consensus was reached on the symbols and their meanings. On-line now, numerous networks collect the surface-weather reports.

Today globally, surface-weather maps indicate that climate warming occurs based on data from local weather stations' very local data. Debate rages about data accuracy from the thousands of worldwide stations.

The graphic below plots present conditions at a local weather station. See www.wpc.ncep.noaa.gov/html/stationplot.shtml

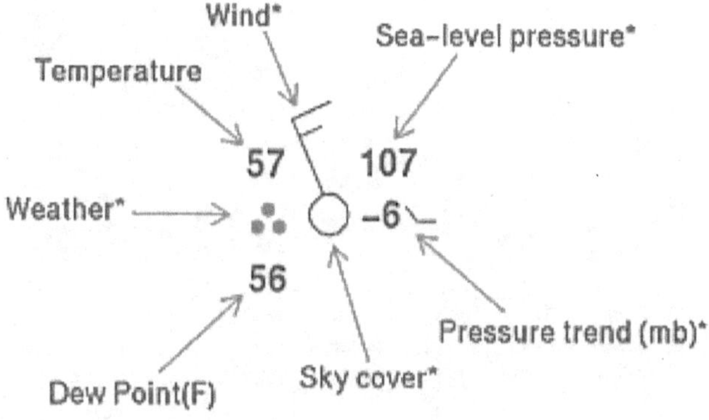
Wind*
Sea-level pressure*
Temperature
57
107
Weather*
-6
56
Pressure trend (mb)*
Sky cover*
Dew Point(F)

RAIN VIOLENT

I

WEATHER STATION ON TOP OF A MOUNTAIN

Ants stream like red monks lining up
to collect sweet from whatever heat
rises and from everything tongue-pretty
with nectar in winter's slip into warming.

RAIN SLIGHT

First we take Manhattan, then Berlin,
maybe Bangkok or Dubai. We infect you;
we swarming, our genes a kaleidoscope
twisting faster than your magnifying eye.

RAIN CONTINUOUS

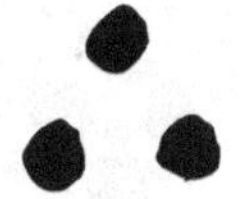

I wear rain gear always.
Some of us go naked, cycling
through the market. Everyone wears
shower caps, crinkling over coiled hair.

RAIN HEAVY

The rain runs the gully, hesitates
in pools, courses on, gathering
our detritus. Inside, children learn,
moving cursors, cut-and-pasting data.

DRIZZLE SLIGHT

Our news on paper remade from shreds,
cleansed with caustics, printed in soy inks,
recycled headlines bleeding, again:
polio Palestine dust and dead water.

DRIZZLE CONTINUOUS

, ,

Climbing the mountain, children flip
two-man rocks, exposing undersides
laced with grubs and white threads. *Flora?*
Fauna? They'll be something, they concur.

DRIZZLE THICK

,
,
,

Mary loses her face first, Jesus
last. The pieta erodes to a curve
holding an agony. Rain dissolves
Golgotha's small wounds.

DRIZZLE THICK FREEZING

No berries, thus no bear rising
from the thicket, no awe at Ursa
circling the North Star. No Goldilocks
at my door with fattened bear stories.

SNOW GRANULAR

Dead and dying bumblebees rain
from 50 Linden trees, newly sprayed
in the big-box parking lot. Better
than the Bible and truer, we swear.

ICE PELLETS

What are the blue orbs on the fruit trees?
Apples wrapped in gauze. Too precious
to leave naked to hail's bruising, maggots'
worming, or migrant workers' quick hands.

HAIL SHOWER SOFT

The brown bears, each to a walk-in
cooler, hibernate on the strip-mall's edge.
They come down freely now, our bears.
We name them Fluffy, One-Eye, Thor.

HAIL SHOWER HEAVY

More died with hailstones than the children of Israel slew with the sword. The sun stood still in the heavens. Joshua trees thirst, their water used for the church car wash.

HAIL SHOWER HARD HEAVY

Dead bees, hard as unpopped corn,
stop the Interstate. Stuck, we listen
to the blues, pass the almonds, agreeing
"You could fry an egg on the pavement."

SNOW FRESH ON GROUND SLIGHT

Flutter on the branch, a rush of finches
beaking off cherry blossoms. We move
our picnic, ourselves, and generations
north for this faint pinking against blue.

SNOW THAWING ON GROUND MODERATE

Summits bare; glaciers melt back.
We can no longer choose ice
over fire, disrobe, fold our rags,
kneel naked, and be assured.

SNOWFLAKES CONTINUOUS

We melted snow. Yes, we drank
ice worms, red threads in our camp cups.
Yes, our breath formed small clouds; yes,
glaciers opened for us, crevasses moaning.

II

WEATHER STATION ON A PLAIN

My dad discovers gold in an aerosol can.
Like Midas, he gilds all. The ozone thins.
I ride my golden bike, my skin bronzing
under the sun's ultraviolet rays.

CALM

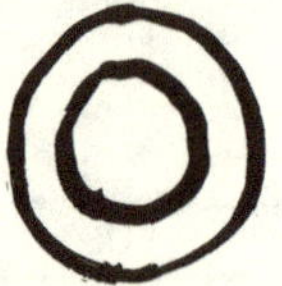

Cascading before the so few things,
heavy with adjectives in the diminishing
diversity: *a crowd, a host, of golden
daffodils... flash upon that inward eye.*

GLORY

Woody Guthrie travels on fresh tar,
singing *Roll on, Columbia, roll* the heavy
sun across the high deserts, buckling freeways,
and dams crumbling as the Great Rivers dry.

MIRAGE

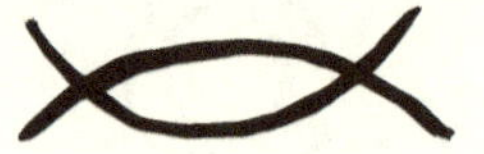

Out of the scrub, children in red T-shirts
run chasing America like a soccer ball.
Border guns collect boys with little sisters.
Mama said walk north, night, star bright.

VISIBILITY REDUCED BY SMOKE

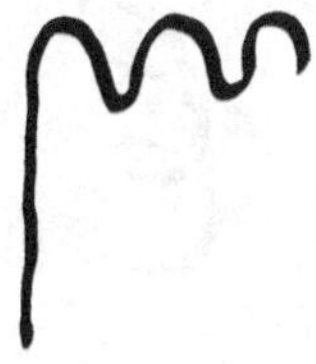

Shooting stars burn through our air,
boil the sea, and fire the forests,
filling the wind with steam and ash.
The horizon is as close as our hands.

DUST DEVIL

Low and hard and dry wind picks
up insects. The air is pitted with body parts
clicking and bumping. Broken ants leak
a mist of formic acid; our eyes sting.

DUST RAISED BY WIND

In Dakotas' tall-grass prairies, Pasque
flowers dim as coal rides the rails
west, bound for China. Our sunsets dull,
a mustard smog rides the westerlies back.

DUST STORM SEVERE

Bison shot, and their dung now dust.
At the Buffalo Chip Toss, giggling teens
fling Idaho spuds, and a Cherokee executes
a hoop dance among the paling camas.

CLOUDS FORMING

All year, the Dog Days of Summer.
Our hounds run in packs, urine claiming
where coyote was and wolf wasn't.
Noon, all three crowd my back stoop.

SKY UNCHANGED

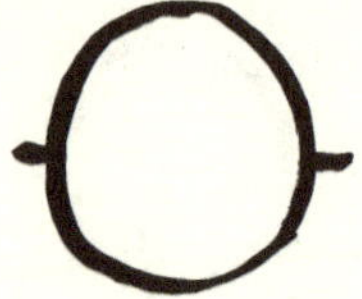

Night soil. The nuns warn us to not eat
migrant strawberries, flats stacked, melting
in the late day. Dawn climbs each furrow,
reddening what is ripe, ready, now.

CLOUDS DISSOLVING

Faucets dry. Streams silent. Pools
fill with brush. I spit on my finger tips
to wash black oil from my child's knees.
From the air drop dead birds.

LIGHTNING, NO THUNDER

Lightning is a beast cracking
through the floor, raking the walls,
coiling brilliantly among us. No Tesla
to break its back into something else.

THUNDER HEARD

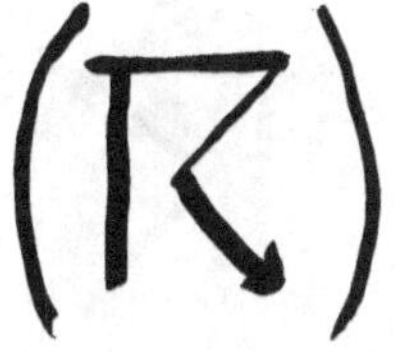

Snake skins, shunting in the wind like riffs
from a broken guitar. Snakes too starved
to rattle, hang from bushes to beat the heat.
We toe the dead with fancy cowboy boots.

THUNDER WITH DUST STORM

I use his ballot to scoop yellow jackets
out the window. I go on line to cast
his vote, but an electrical storm fries
the clicks cast into cyberspace. Boom.

THUNDER WITH RAIN HEAVY

Dropped out of a downpour, snow geese winter in the inundated fields, webbed feet compacting soil. Farmers fire into the flood of cackling. Wings undulate across the flats.

THUNDER WITH RAIN/SNOW

November's big wind. Finding the candles. Small movements in a dark house. Do you have a match? Know how to strike a match? Surely you know how to make fire?

ICE NEEDLES

Chicken Little, on its freezer tray
labeled *hatchd, raisd, harvestd US*,
wasn't sent to China to be butchered,
flash frozen, eaten Fresh Off the Boat.

SNOW BLOWING

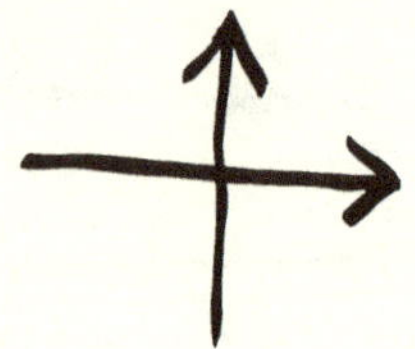

From snow, animals dig bunchgrass.
Narcissa Whitman covers the table
with a white cloth, no matter the news.
In time, gone the cloth, the bunchgrass.

III

WEATHER STATION IN A DEEP VALLEY

The pope's bee decorates the world map
surveyed from sailing ships, continents
misshapen. Satellites map the earth,
down to the monk's inadequate roof.

WINDS VARIABLE

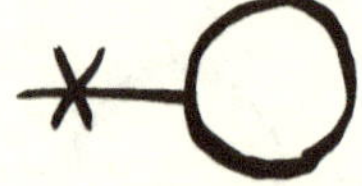

I count birds at dusk, enough light.
Flocking, chickadees liven the twigs.
warm breast and with ah! bright wings.
Gusts, and anything loose lifts.

WIND OUT OF THE SOUTHWEST

Barometer falling. Narcissus with broken stems lost in the wet grass, and Parnassian butterflies grounded among the folded leaves of Hawkbit and Bleeding Heart. We tap the glass again.

WIND OUT OF THE NORTH

Earth's magnetic field reverses.
The Compass Rose mutates, and true
north is false. Electronic hearts skitter.
Data, like confused fighter jets, scramble.

25 MPH WIND OUT OF THE NORTH WITH GUSTS

Salal brushes my ankles, and farther on,
I hear my pocket change clink. There is no
silence in trying to get away. In the clearings,
the strange grass accepts the wind's push.

SQUALL

Wind scours pollen from the cherry blooms;
ten thousand years of hybridizing gone.
Fickle wind mixes this and its unlike-that.
We are out there with our Q-tips, trying.

SQUALL LINE

Garden tour. In each SUV
two aunties, one driving, one
riding shotgun. Gallon jars, loose
oolong floats in each. Sun tea.

FUNNEL CLOUD

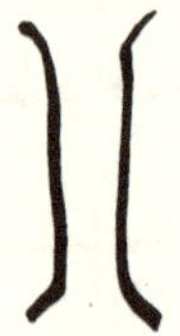

In the no-cock zone, GMO-fed
chicks turn rooster, strutting toward
an inexpert beheading. Jesus goes first,
then Jesus II, into a tough coq au vin.

HURRICANE

Our neighbor got the heavy stuff: roof
and BBQ; the main drag got the dog
and chickens, some running mid air.
Flung on trees, our resolve now tinsel.

TROPICAL STORM

The wind comes from the wrong direction.
Our drains reverse. Every straight tree
gives over, lichen scattering like neon
confetti. Root discs block our retreat.

TURBULENCE HEAVY

My friend texts me on his flight to China
that the plane's belly holds ten thousand
live chickens, their return booked on ice.
Two roosters strut the aisle, tidbitting.

IV

WEATHER STATION ON A COAST

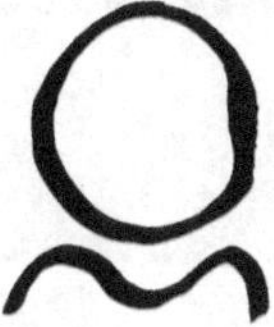

We forget how a sea can be.
No wind taps the waves into crests.
No crests break on the steepened beach.
No northering velella towing spring.

DUMPING GROUND

I gut my sea duck; trinkets fall out.
Microbeads nest in fish flesh.
The Garbage Patch sheds jetsam
from its gyre of the little that floats.

GROUND FLOODED

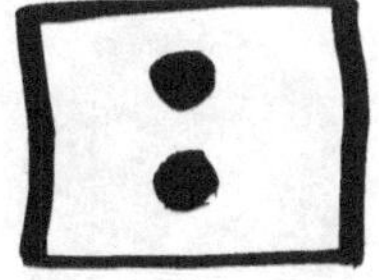

Ice clinks in my drink, and honey settles
through the cubes like quickened gold; vodka
heats my throat. An unebbing tide surrounds
my beach chair. I can't afford to move.

SKY OVERCAST

Blind, she brings home stones pried
from the rocky beach. She steams them. No
low-tide scent rises, no clams crackle open.
She thinks her sense of smell now lost.

NO CLOUDS

The high, blue ice gone, melt
gone, saltwater intruding, salmon
shallowing across the flood plain, arching
backbones, skittering across the pavement.

SKY OBSCURED
SMOKE, DUST, SULFUR DIOXIDE

He kills his wife. She leaves her hand
too long in the neighbor's grip helping
her from the boat. He kills his enemy, son,
father, dog and all the others for less.

FOG SHALLOW

Paris. Coyotes arrive, vague among
the footfalls and cats skirting the edge,
streets with no exit. Boxed in, coyotes
go to ground, waiting *au sous sol*.

FOG SHALLOW PATCHY

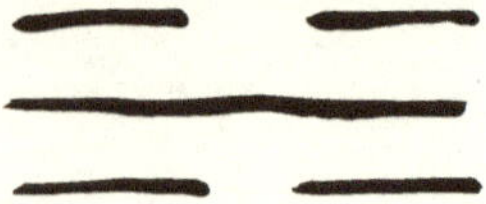

Stress, they say. White feathers mark
the black crows' wings; soon all
white, pecking bleached seaweed
on the vacated beach, done as tricksters.

FOG SHALLOW LESS THAN SIX FEET DEEP

Stone walls, warm as the palms lifting
each rock, hot as the blood staining them.
Either side turns neutral ground, defenses
crumble, stones stolen for other walls.

FOG DEPOSITING RIME

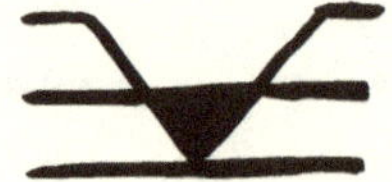

West across the Aleutians, coyotes move,
loitering in the killing fields, mating with
the Golden Jackal, Starving Buddha's dog,
and สุนัขจิ้งจอก (sòo-nák jîng-jòk).

DRIZZLE NOT FREEZING

The moon's ragged edge rasps dusk.
We walk out into the field of wet.
Our garden's last cut. Mint or cane
or nettle. Grief in every handful.

DRIZZLE THICK CONTINUOUS

In the park's backwater, the green river
and its few cattails share mud
with bodies and the final frogs.
Children and poets climb parallel bars.

RAIN FREEZING SLIGHT

Nettles collapsing in the long loss.
Winter wrens quiet their soft sing. Rain
silvering blue iris, and the crow's cra'ack
recedes. What Tiresias saw was this.

RAIN FREEZING HEAVY

It rains sorrow. We wait for the grandmas
to die and mothers to die who search
for sons and cut daughters. We wait
for babies born blind to the guttered blood.

RAIN VIOLENT

They on the shore are not us. In the rain,
they set their boats on fire. Wood ignites;
the plastics smoke, black and acrid. To slake
thirst, they open their mouths, faces up.

SNOW CRYSTALS STARLIKE

Out of the boat, kindness steps.
She is pregnant, full. She has done this
before, stepping out of boats, rocking,
finding balance, grasping the bird's tail.

ABOUT ANN SPIERS

Ann Spiers lives on Vashon Island, Puget Sound, where she was the island's inaugural poet laureate. Her diverse life provides the seeds for *Rain Violent's* quatrains. She raised sons down trail in a beach cabin, leads writing workshops, assists with fieldwork in the Cascade volcanoes and for citizen science projects, and hiked the Washington coast from the Columbia River to Cape Flattery.

Her poems appear widely in journals, anthologies, and online. In addition to *Rain Violent* (Empty Bowl), other volumes published in 2021 are *Back Cut* (Black Heron) and *Harpoon* (Triplet Series, Ravenna).

Her chapbooks include *What Rain Does* (Egress Studio), *Bunker Trail* (Finishing Line), and *Long Climb into Grace* (FootHills). Letterpress editions of *The Herodotus Poems* (Brooding Heron) and *Volcano Blue, Tide Turn,* and *A Wild Taste* (May Day) are in the Special Collections at the U. of Washington, Stanford, British Library, Multnomah County Library, University of Puget Sound, and Bainbridge Island Museum of Art.

At the U. of Washington, she earned a MA in English Lit and Creative Writing and an Environmental Manager Certificate. She writes interpretive signage for natural history museums, land trusts, and parks. As staff, she compiled acquisition baselines for the local land trust and park district. Her Vashon trail guide is a best seller.

annspiers.com

ABOUT BOLINAS FRANK

Visual artist Bolinas Frank was born in Seattle, grew up on Vashon Island, and is now living in Seoul.

For *Rain Violent*, he first painted the weather symbols with brush. He then, through a digital process, forged a font, a collection comprised of each image.

His training in visual art started at 3 years old under the direction of many studio artists. This early mentorship included Seattle's Pratt Fine Arts Center where Samaj taught him to be fearless through the understanding and feel of materials. He received a BFA in studio art at the U. of Arizona with training from artists Robert Colescott, Bailey Doogan, Alfred Quiroz, Chuck Hitner, and Harmony Hammond.

Bolinas sees the painting surface as a skin, and his creation emerges on the intelligent edge where art and life interface. Through his painting's stacked messages, he asks what is underneath things, what is on the hidden side, what secrets lie underneath, and what information asserts itself. He moves the importance of materials and process away from a purely isolated authoritative state of representation and toward the realm of expression. His work speaks about migration, domesticity, atrophy, exposing underlying flaws and defects that are carried, delivered, and exposed.

His artwork is in private collections in Europe, Asia, and across America with notable shows in the Hardened Artery, Gallery 110, OK Hotel, Valise, Columbia Center, and Little Uncle.

Connect with Bolinas at linktr.ee/bolinas

www.ingramcontent.com/pod-product-compliance
Lightning Source LLC
La Vergne TN
LVHW051015080826
845145LV00009B/2634

* 9 7 8 1 7 3 4 1 8 7 3 9 7 *